JOB SEARCH MASTERY

*How to obliterate obstacles on
the path to your next job*

Marsha E. Friedman

Copyright © 2020, Marsha E. Friedman.

All rights reserved.

No part of this book may be reproduced or transmitted in any form or by any means, electronic or mechanical, including photocopying, recording, or by any information retrieval system, without permission in writing from the publisher.

Writing & Publishing Process by David James

Book Cover Design by David James

Edited by Amber J. Chapman | AJCcopywritingediting.com

ISBN: 979-8-5548970-9-2

Disclaimer: This book contains opinions, ideas, experiences, and exercises. The purchaser and/or reader of these materials assumes all responsibility for the use of this information. Marsha E. Friedman and Publisher assume no responsibility and/or liability whatsoever for any purchaser and/or reader of these materials.

CONTENTS

Introduction v

Chapter 1 – Job Search Success: *It Starts with You!* 1

Chapter 2 - Take a Time-Out: *Check Your Attitude* 21

Chapter 3 – Stand Out: *Increase your Value* 43

Chapter 4 – Build Momentum: *Action Brings Success* 57

Summary 71

Appendix A – Recommended Books 73

Appendix B – 5 Tips To Combat Ageism 83

Appendix C - Job Search Groups across the US 87

Acknowledgments 95

References 97

About the Author 99

INTRODUCTION

You are a job seeker. Whether you were laid off, furloughed, quit, or asked to leave. You brushed yourself off, updated your resume, and started your job search. You are networking, answering job ads, talking to recruiters, and so far, no luck.

As time passes, you will face (or are already facing):

- pressures from home, especially from a spouse or significant other
- emotions running the gamut from hope to hopelessness
- the challenge of maintaining momentum when you didn't make the cut or get the offer you anticipated
- your own negative attitudes and self-doubts
- the difficulty of getting out of your head and out of your own way

The personal (emotional) side of the job search doesn't get the attention that the transactional (practical) side does (resumes, interviewing, networking, branding, social media, etc.). There are hundreds of articles, websites, videos, and how-to manuals to help you craft a resume, develop a marketing plan, network like a pro, and negotiate your starting salary and benefits.

This book is unique in its devotion to the soft side of the search. *Job Search Mastery* fills in the gaps between the transactional and personal sides of the job search by taking a holistic approach to the job search journey. In this book you will discover the strategies, tools, and exercises to help you manage the physical, emotional, and psychological side of the job search.

Chapter 1 – Job Search Success: It Starts with You!

This chapter is centered on you, the job seeker. How are you caring for yourself: emotionally and physically? What changes and adjustments can you make to bring more balance into your life? How can you improve your self-image and your self-confidence? How are you treating your body? How are you preparing your best self to show up to the interview and your new job? If you want to stand out from other candidates, start by evaluating your self-care and making the necessary adjustments to put yourself first.

Chapter 2 – Take a Time-Out: Check Your Attitude

This chapter asks you to consider your state of mind. Is your glass half-empty or half-full? How will your attitude impact the outcome of your interviews? What factors influence your attitude? How can you control those factors? Who are the people in your inner circle and how does their outlook impact yours? How can you surround yourself with support?

Chapter 3 – Stand Out: How to Become an Asset to Potential Employers

This chapter will challenge you to expand your expertise and keep your skills sharp. As the length of your search grows, how will you address questions that arise about employment gaps? If you are changing careers or industries, do you have the necessary knowledge and skills to make that change? What can you do to stay current in your industry? What are you using as conversation starters in interviews and networking meetings?

Chapter 4 – Build Momentum: Action Brings Success

This chapter is about gaining traction in your job search. What actions can you take to keep your search moving forward? How can you maximize your time and energy? How can you maintain forward momentum when you encounter a negative action? What and whom are your sources of support? How do you ask for help? What are the pros and cons of accepting contract or project work?

Within each chapter, you will find sidebars that explore selected topics more deeply as well as tips, exercises, and strategies to help you embrace positivity and, ultimately, succeed in your job search. To begin, read the questions posed in each chapter, then start where you are — in the chapter that has the answers you are seeking today.

My hope is that *Job Search Mastery* brings you the essential guidance and support you need to break through the challenges awaiting you on your job search journey.

CHAPTER 1
JOB SEARCH SUCCESS:
It Starts with You!

"He who knows others is wise; he who knows himself is enlightened."

—Lao-Tzu

In the spring of 2014, armed with a stellar 30+-year employment track record and a newly minted master's degree in hand (with a 4.0 GPA), I knew it was just *one giant leap* to my dream job! I was confident that I'd be snapped up immediately, offered increased leadership responsibilities with a six-figure salary, and amazing benefits. Or, so I thought…

I soon realized that I was just one of many people with similar credentials who had no guarantee of a shortcut in the job search process. My sprint quickly turned into a marathon. My takeaway was that landing a job today takes time, energy, research, concentration, and networking, as well as perseverance and resilience.

You will have a head start on other candidates if you think of your job search as a marathon rather than a sprint! Consider the preparations that a first-time marathon runner must undertake. Being a successful marathoner requires evaluating and testing your endurance, learning about and selecting the best equipment as well as building strength and developing perseverance. It is a head-to-toe endeavor and so is the job search.

This chapter challenges you to evaluate your emotional and physical fitness for the job-search marathon ahead. Emotional fitness is the capacity to handle the emotional ups and downs that come with the job search process through healthy habits and practices. Physical fitness during the job search translates to flexibility, endurance, and agility. Being physically fit will help you avoid stress, be more self-confident, and ward off fatigue.

Creating a Roadmap

You have likely been working for a number of years – on that rinse-and-repeat cycle of getting up, eating breakfast, brushing your teeth, getting dressed and going to work, and then coming home, having dinner, watching TV or reading, taking a shower, going to bed and starting all over again in the morning. Rinse and repeat, daily. When have you been blessed with the time to focus on yourself?

As a job seeker, take advantage of the time you have right now to pause and reevaluate your life. A good starting point is a "life balance wheel" (aka "Wheel of Life") exercise. The life balance wheel invites you to rate your satisfaction across eight aspects of your personal and professional life. Balance wheels enable you to quickly identify where you are, where you want to go, and your priorities for moving forward.

In each segment of the balance wheel, circle the number that most closely represents your level of personal satisfaction (with 1 being the lowest and 7 being the highest).

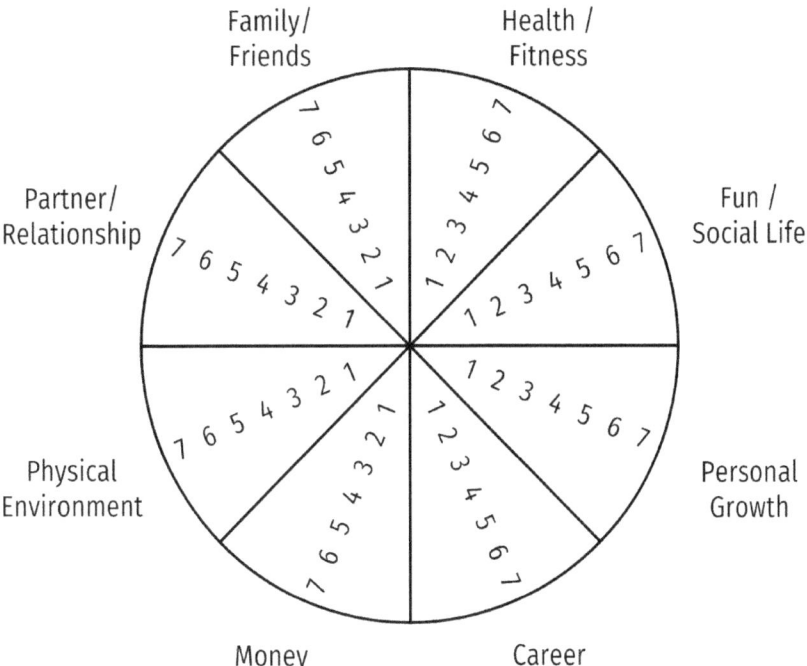

Now draw a line across the number you circled and connect each of the eight lines around the wheel. Color in each section of your balance wheel and ask yourself these questions:

- If my life balance wheel were on a car, what kind of ride would I experience? Smooth or rocky?
- How do you feel about your life as you look at your wheel? Are there any surprises?

- Which categories would you most like to improve?
- What small changes can you make to smooth out your ride and bring more balance into your life?
- How could I make space for these changes? What support and help might I need from others to make these changes?
- If there were one key action I could take that would begin to bring everything into balance, what would it be?

Your completed balance wheel is your roadmap to designing the life that you want with harmony between your personal and professional lives. The balance wheel helps you to recognize that your career is just one component of a full life.

The information you glean from this exercise can have an impact on the job you accept. For example, if one of your goals is to create more family time, then you might not want to take a job that requires an increase in your commute or in overnight travel. Additionally, if personal growth is a key to your satisfaction, then the organization's culture around learning and development may weigh as heavily on your decision making as your salary and benefits package.

Another tool to help you evaluate your fitness for the job search journey ahead is the Self Care Quiz. Think of it as a head-to-toe scan of your personal care practices. The results of your Self Care Quiz will highlight areas that could use some maintenance and attention. Consider this exercise as a tune-up for your body and soul.

SELF-CARE QUIZ

INSTRUCTIONS

How good are you to yourself? Let's find out! Know that there are no right or wrong answers, just answer however seems appropriate for you right now and see what you learn about yourself.

	yes	sometimes	no
I am up-to-date with my doctor, dentist, and other health check-ups.	☐	☐	☐
I am happy with my physical fitness and energy levels.	☐	☐	☐
I eat well (nutritionally) most of the time.	☐	☐	☐
I do not abuse my body with caffeine, alcohol, or other stimulants.	☐	☐	☐
I get plenty of sleep so I usually feel well rested.	☐	☐	☐
I take regular breaks from my work during the day.	☐	☐	☐
I use my weekends and vacations for enjoyment and relaxation.	☐	☐	☐
I am comfortable with my "style" (hairstyle, wardrobe, etc.).	☐	☐	☐
I prioritize how I spend my time and important things get done on time.	☐	☐	☐

	Yes	Sometimes	No
I say "No" to others and myself when I need to.	☐	☐	☐
My home is a calm haven (or has a place within it) that takes me away from the stresses of the world.	☐	☐	☐
I recognize my stress signals and know when to take a break.	☐	☐	☐
I have people in my life who love and support me.	☐	☐	☐
I spend most of my time with people who encourage, energize, and inspire me.	☐	☐	☐
I listen to and trust my intuition when it comes to taking care of myself.	☐	☐	☐

TOTAL SCORE
(2x each Yes, 1x each Sometimes, 0 for each No) ___ ___ ___

The maximum possible total is 30. **Write your total score here** _____

If your score is 26 or above, you are paying attention to those things that matter and taking the time to renew and refresh yourself. Bravo! Give yourself a pat on the back! With a few small tweaks, you can have a perfect score.

If your score is between 15 and 25, you are halfway there! For each "no" or "sometimes" answer, jot down one small action that you could take to improve your score. Then, choose the action that will have the greatest impact on your self-care. With that action completed, work your way through the list one small change at a time. If you need encouragement, inspiration, or support, share your plans with your spouse or a friend and ask him/her to hold you accountable for making positive changes.

If your score is below 15, the stress of the job search will only add to your anxiety and frustration and you may be headed for a crisis. Take a hard look at each "no" or "sometimes" answer and ask yourself what habits or beliefs are getting in your way?

It's time to take a deep breath and a step back, and ask for help from a coach. A coach can help you look at limiting beliefs, self-sabotaging habits, your lifestyle, and values. With their help, you will identify the small changes that can have an immediate impact.

Even if your time and energy are limited, your coach can help you set short-term goals that will enable you to be more present and more productive as you begin your job search journey.

Embrace Your Emotions

As someone who has been laid off or furloughed, forced to quit, or has been fired, you know how shocking, devastating, and demoralizing this event can be. You talk about the anger, hurt, and sadness you felt—and how your life was turned upside down. You remember the sleepless nights filled with tossing, turning, and worrying about finances. You can still feel the urge to lash out at the world.

At the same time, you know that despite years of success, this one moment made you feel like a complete and utter failure. You say that you lost your sense of identity and along with it your "tribe" of coworkers and friends. You wake up in the morning with no plans and no sense of purpose. You are knee-deep in grief.

When you are going through any major life change including a job loss, you will experience all of the phases of the grief cycle: denial, anger, bargaining, depression, and acceptance.

There is no timeline or even any order for how we go through the phases of grief. Some phases can happen simultaneously, or we can move back and forth between the stages of grief. That movement can be quick or slow. The grief process for each person is as unique as we are. It varies based on the change with which we are struggling and our internal and external support systems.

> ### The Five Phases of Grief
>
> Regardless of which life-change we face, the bumpy road from denial to acceptance is the same. You will run through the full gamut of the grief cycle as defined by Elizabeth Kubler-Ross, MD, in her book, *On Death and Dying*. Here's a summary of the five-phase grief cycle:
>
> **1. Denial:** Not accepting what has happened puts us in a state of shock and denial; we are stunned, overwhelmed, and numb. Nothing makes sense anymore. This phase enables us to get through our struggles one day at a time.

2. Anger: In this phase, we project anger at anyone and anything, even the universe. We lash out at the world, anyone who disagrees with our view, and anything that upsets our day. Anger provides a framework to channel our frustration and despair in the face of loss. This emotion gives us strength of purpose and a path to survival.

3. Bargaining: This is the phase where we look at all of the "if onlys" and "what ifs" to wish for a different outcome. We attempt to bargain for an alternate reality rather than the one we are facing. We explore all of the things we could have done differently and wallow in the guilt of the "if onlys." There is never one "if only" or "what if," we must process the full range of options to accept the outcome.

4. Depression: During this phase, we can't or won't get up in the morning. We feel sad and lethargic, and we cry or want to cry. We feel hopeless and lost, have trouble sleeping or sleep too much. We don't want to eat or we eat and/or drink too much. In other words, we are out of balance. This depression is not a form of mental illness but an appropriate response to loss and a natural part of the healing process.

5. Acceptance: During this final phase, we make peace with the loss and start moving on with life. We accept the new reality of life, the new normal. We adjust to new surroundings, new relationships, and new daily patterns. We are capable of accepting our feelings, responding to our own needs, and engaging with the world again.

The job search process puts you on a roller coaster of emotional ups and downs. When you get an interview or phone screen, you are excited and hopeful, but when you get a rejection, you are anxious and sad. How far up or down your emotions carry you and how long you stay up or down is completely unique to you. But, get your seat belt on, you are in for a bumpy ride.

In order to smooth out your ride, open yourself completely to your emotions. Let yourself feel the full range of emotions that you are experiencing. Those emotions can fluctuate from the depths of despair, feeling scared, anxious, and hopeless to the heights of elation, excitement, contentment, and joy. Emotional fitness is the capacity to handle the emotional ups and downs of the job search process through healthy habits and practices.

If you find yourself feeling low and stuffing emotions back down, watch out! This practice could backfire in the long run. When you release those pent up negative emotions, chances are good that you will lash out at your loved ones or take unnecessary risks (drinking, eating, spending money, binge watching, etc.).

What are our negative emotions telling us? How do we react to what we are feeling? According to speaker and author of *Untamed*, Glennon Doyle, our feelings are our guides leading us to do the next right thing.

For example, if you are feeling the emotion on the left in the chart below, consider taking the action on the right:

EMOTION	ACTION
Overwhelmed	Ask for help
Pain	Help others
Lonely	Get connected
Angry	Search your heart
Anxious	Uncover your fears
Defeated	Focus on what you've learned

The next time one of these painful feelings comes over you, let go of that emotion by looking for the action that it brings (Doyle, 2013).

Here's how to discover that action:

1. Take a few deep breaths, then listen with your whole heart to the answer you hold inside.
2. Be open and curious to allow the answers to come into your awareness.
3. Let that answer set your intentions and guide your actions.

If you don't hear the answer, journaling may help in the discovery and healing process.

Journaling 101

What is journaling? Simply stated, journaling is the practice of capturing your thoughts, experiences, and observations about your life and your world on paper. Journaling has no rules. The key is to just write and let your thoughts go where they will.

What's the purpose of journaling? The purpose of journaling is to clear the thoughts from your head. No matter how scattered or unstructured your writing might seem, the act of just getting words down on paper enables you to have a conversation with yourself. When you are stuck on an issue and you are mulling it over in your head, you are problem-storing. Journaling extends the discussion and opens the path to problem solving.

What are the benefits of journaling?

- Journaling can help you create order when your world feels like it's in chaos.
- Journaling can help you uncover your fears, thoughts, and feelings.
- Journaling can help you think through problems or challenges.
- Journaling can help you visualize your future.
- Journaling can help you manage change.
- Journaling can help you settle disputes or resolve conflicts.
- Journaling can help you figure out your next steps or create solutions.
- Journaling can help you take a step back and look at your life with an outsider's view.
- Journaling can help you cope with your emotions, giving you a safe space to vent.

- Journaling can help you unleash your creativity.
- Journaling can help you understand the connections between thoughts, feelings and actions.
- Journaling can help you appreciate simple blessings.
- Journaling can help you reduce stress.
- Journaling can help you live a healthier, happier life.

Here's what you need to get started:

What: Paper and pens/pencils. Use a notebook, loose-leaf paper, stationary, or buy a journal. Use any pen/pencil that feels good in your hand. Try tri-colored pens or pencils or use a variety of pens/pencils.

When: You can journal anytime that works for you: mornings, evenings, weekdays, weekends, daily, weekly, monthly. You can write at a specific time every day, write when you have time, or when you have something you want to work out.

Where: You can journal anywhere at home or out — your bedroom, your living room, your office, a coffee shop, or a park. Simply find a quiet space, take a few deep breaths (inhaling to the count of 5 and out to the count of 5), and write! Note: Once you decide where you will write, place your journal and your pens in an easily accessible spot.

How: Write long hand. There is something visceral and emotional in the act of writing. The connection between brain and hand is an amazing learning tool. Don't worry — handwriting and spelling don't count, and no one else is going to read what you wrote.

Rules: There are no rules in journaling. Write where and when the mood strikes you. Use whatever helps you express yourself: words, pictures, photographs, doodles, poems, articles, quotes, drawings – anything that helps you to sort through your thoughts and feelings. "Turning feelings into words can help us process and overcome adversity" (Sandberg & Grant 62).

Writing prompts: If you need inspiration to begin writing, Google "journal prompts" and a variety of suggestions will be at your fingertips; from one-word prompts to top-ten lists to questions and quotes. Prompts are everywhere. Some journals include daily prompts, too.

The key to journaling is to begin…Commit now to your next steps.

1. Day/date I will start: _____
2. Time I will start: _____
3. Location I will use: _____
4. Paper and pen I will use: _____

To learn more about the practice of journaling, check out these sites:

- Julia Cameron, author of *The Artist's Way*, a book that guides its readers on a journey to creativity, discusses the use of morning pages.[1]
- The Daily Stoic[2] provides the scientific benefits, history and

---

[1] https://juliacameronlive.com/basic-tools/morning-pages/

[2] https://dailystoic.com/journaling/

detailed guidance on the practice of journaling.

Exercise - A Dozen Simple Things to do When Your Emotions are Out of Control

If your negative emotions such as anger, fear, frustration, or sadness are weighing you down, try one of these activities to lighten your mood and improve your outlook:

- Yell into a pillow or start a pillow fight
- Listen to calming music
- Read
- Start your day with meditation
- Take a time out to slow your breathing to help calm and center yourself
- Exercise
- Write in a journal
- Phone a friend
- Watch a sad, scary, or funny movie
- Pet your cat or dog
- Do something nice for someone else — get your attention off of yourself and your worries
- Write a letter to get the emotion out, then you can tuck the letter away for a while (or forever), tear it up, or burn it. Whatever you decide to do, don't sign it or send it. The purpose of this exercise is to simply release yourself from the negative thoughts and emotions.

Physical Fitness: Inside & Out

Physical fitness is critical to your job search. In order to be at your best, ask yourself if you are doing the most you can for your body, both inside and out.

- How well are your feeding yourself?
- Are you overindulging in sweets, alcohol, or caffeine?
- How many servings of fruits and vegetables do you eat every day?
- Do you have a balanced approach to exercise? Too much, like an exercise fanatic? Or too little, like a happy couch potato?

Diet and exercise are closely related. How well we nourish our bodies is as important as how we maintain our physical endurance.

If you want to stand out from other candidates and present your best self, you will want to power your body with nutritious foods. We can survive by eating almost any type of food. But if we want to thrive, we must become conscious of what we are putting into our mouths, how often we eat, and the quality of the ingredients we use. As we age, this becomes even more critical.

No one can dictate how you should eat, that's your decision. But please give some serious thought to how you fuel your engine. Start slowly by paying attention to how you feel before and after every meal.

To help you begin this practice, here is a simple eight-question Daily Food & Emotions Chart. Make copies of this chart, carry it with you for a full week and fill it out before and after every snack or meal.

At the end of the week, review your entries for patterns of thinking and eating that may not be serving you well. Once you recognize your challenges with eating then ask yourself what you could you do differently. Choose one small change to begin — then repeat this exercise to eliminate other eating challenges.

DAILY FOOD & EMOTIONS CHART

Breakfast	Lunch	Snack #1	Dinner	Snack #2
Before you eat a snack or a meal, rate your level of hunger on a scale of 1 to 5, with 1 being not hungry and 5 being ravenous					
Why am I eating? a) I'm hungry, b) it's time to eat, c) to be social, d) other					
What's my emotional state?					
The food that I'm about to eat is: a) fuel for energy, b) comfort food, c) quick & easy, d) what's served					
After the meal, rate your level of satiation: a) satisfied, b) mild fullness, c) uncomfortably full, d) stuffed, e) physically ill					
Do I need or want more food? Yes or No					
What food would satisfy my hunger?					
Did this meal give me the physical energy/mental clarity I need? Yes or No					

Clean Eating

Consider getting processed food and sugar out of your house and eating at home more often. Processed food contain high levels of sugar often hidden in the list of ingredients. There are things like corn syrup, glucose, fructose, and maltodextrin to name a few. In addition, chain restaurants are serving us foods engineered with salt and sugar to make them more palatable and enticing so that we overeat. Based on the obesity rates in this country the chain restaurants and processed food manufacturers are quite successful with their marketing and product development endeavors.

Try eating a diet that is high in protein, fresh fruits and vegetables, and healthy fats. When you fuel your body with healthy unprocessed food you feel and look better. Your skin glows, your gut is happy, and you have more energy and mental clarity. Studies by the National Institute of Health (Burfoot, 2019) have shown that people who eat processed foods consume considerably more calories and gain more weight than those who eat a diet of unprocessed foods.

While you may not be able to make all these changes at one time, just start small. What is one baby step you can take to improve your diet?

Here are some ideas:

- Eliminate sugary desserts and eat fruit instead
- Try one new vegetable every week
- Add one healthy snack a day

Swap out soda and drink tap or sparkling water with lemon

Exercise will help you manage stress, feel more self-confident, and reduce fatigue. When we are physically active, our bodies release endorphins, the hormones that help us manage stress. Even a moderate amount of exercise such as walking 20 minutes a day 3 times per week will provide these benefits. The key is to choose an exercise that you enjoy and is easy to get started: walking, hiking, biking, swimming, running, etc. Another bonus is that exercise will help you sleep better, feel more rested, and increase your energy levels.

If you are a job seeker who is concerned about age discrimination in the hiring process, then get up off the couch and get moving! A regular program of exercise will keep you looking younger, improve your self-image, and boost your self-confidence. By maintaining a healthy weight and keeping your body fit, employers will be less likely to view your age as a negative factor in the selection process. More importantly, with a revitalized self-image, you will present yourself as a stronger, more dynamic candidate.

> *"You may not control all the events that happen to you, but you can decide not to be reduced by them."*
>
> —Maya Angelou

Chapter 2
TAKE A TIME-OUT:
Check Your Attitude

"What seems to us as bitter trials are often blessings in disguise."

—Oscar Wilde

What does your persona say about you? Not sure? Come with me to the land of Winnie the Pooh and the Hundred Acre Wood to meet two of the most popular characters who live there. Eeyore, the donkey, sees the world through a cloudy lens of "woe is me," while Tigger, the tiger, bounces through life with a carefree, happy-go-lucky attitude. Which character would your friends and family say is most like you?

Why do I ask? I ask, because whether you realize it or not, your attitude is your calling card while you're in a job search. When you are on the phone, your persona comes through in your voice. Your voice carries with it your emotions, your attitude, and your energy. Who are prospective employers and networking contacts encountering? Before you dial a number, answer a call, or jump on a video, think about who is picking up the phone or clicking the link. Consciously ask yourself: Who am I right now? Am I being Eeyore or am I a Tigger?

Standing up, walking around, and smiling when you take interview or networking calls will bring out the Tigger in you. Think about this every time you take or make a call, meet with a networking contact, or head into an interview. Being aware of how you are showing up and managing your attitude can shorten the length of your job search.

Mental Fitness & Attitude

Mental fitness is an awareness of the connections between thoughts, feelings, and behaviors, and the ability to manage your thoughts, accept your feelings, and influence your behaviors. Mental fitness gets you out of your head and out of your own way in order to keep your search moving forward.

Have you ever labeled yourself a disappointment, an imposter or a failure and couldn't seem to get that label out of your thoughts? If so, what's behind this behavior? Your thoughts are a catalyst for self-perpetuating cycles. What you think directly influences how you feel and how you behave. Your emotions are the direct connection between thinking and behavior.

This graphic shows how that connection flows:

For example, after being fired or laid off, you might be thinking, "I'm a failure." As a result of this thought, you will feel like a failure and you will act like a failure, which reinforces your belief that you must be a failure. Feel free to substitute whatever negative thought you have about yourself for the word failure (for example: I'm not good enough. I'm an imposter. I'm so stupid!).

Once you draw a negative conclusion about yourself, you are likely to do two things;

- look for evidence to reinforce your belief
- discount anything that runs contrary to your belief

Someone who develops the belief that they're a failure, for example, will view each mistake as proof that they are not good enough. When they do succeed at something, they will chalk it up to luck.

How can you get off this merry-go-round of circular thinking? Try asking yourself questions that will force you to validate your thoughts with fact-based evidence. This exercise comes from Byron Katie's book, *The Work*. Ask yourself these questions to discover the truth:

1. Is it true?
2. How can you absolutely know that it's true?
3. How do you react, what happens, when you believe that thought?
4. Who would you be without that thought?

Going through this exercise will encourage you to think differently, use evidence and facts to back up your conclusions and open your eyes to a new reality.

Exercise: Build Evidence of Your Success

1. Make a list of all of your accomplishments, both business and personal, from making friends on the playground and learning to ride a bike to reducing expenses and receiving awards. Put that list in a sheet protector and carry it with you. Whenever you need a shot of confidence, take it out, read it over, and feel your power.

2. Create a portfolio or brag book[3], which provides validation and documentation to support your resume and LinkedIn profile. Your portfolio can include your resume, marketing plan, samples of your work, educational achievements, awards, letters of recommendation, etc. Your portfolio reinforces what you bring to the workplace, highlights your expertise, and documents your credentials. In an interview, it will set you apart from other candidates and demonstrate your preparedness. Leafing through your portfolio will give you a shot of confidence and boost your self-esteem.

Having a Bad Day?

Does this sound familiar? You have a networking call at 2:00 p.m. today with a C-Level executive from the company you would love to work for

---

[3] https://www.fivestrengths.com/brag-book/

HOWEVER…

You blew this morning's phone screen and to top that off you didn't get the job offer you were expecting. Your disappointment is palpable and your self-confidence is at an all-time low.

OR…

Your unemployment just ran out, your finances are tight, and your spouse is constantly asking about your job search. You feel useless and ashamed.

OR…

Your kids are squabbling over whose turn it is to take the dog for a walk, it's pouring rain, and they have no place to go. The decibel level in your home is reaching a new high, you can't concentrate, and you are struggling to prepare for your meeting. You feel your blood pressure rising and your patience wearing thin. You are angry, frustrated, and scared.

If you are having a particularly challenging day and Eeyore has moved in, don't let a bad attitude limit your opportunities or derail your search. While you can postpone the call to another day and time, consider these rescue strategies to regain forward momentum:

- Review your accomplishments log and/or brag book to renew your confidence.
- Phone your job search partner or coach and talk through your fears and frustrations.

- Take some deep cleansing breaths – inhale to the count of 5 and then exhale to the count of 5 – repeat 5 times to slow your breathing and regain your focus.
- Work through your emotions by journaling to calm your mind.
- Go out for a walk or run as raising endorphins reduces stress level.

If you tried these rescue exercises and your head still isn't in the game, make that call and reschedule the interview or appointment.

Cliff's Story

Cliff reached out to me in a panic. He was in the midst of a series of interviews for a job that was right up his alley. He was feeling confused and asked for help in clearing his thoughts before the final interview of the day. As I listened to Cliff, I posed questions to help him think deeper and to isolate his concerns to make them more manageable.

- The title for this job was "Director," while he had previously held the title of Vice President. The use of titles varies from company to company and the scope of responsibility is the more important factor to consider.
- How does the scope of responsibility and level of authority compare to your previous position?
- What opportunities for growth do you foresee in this job?
- The job could not be done remotely and might require relocation.

- What flexibility, if any, does the employer have?
- Would it be possible to commute each week, spending weekends at home?
- Cliff admitted that he was still grappling with the emotional issues of his layoff.
- How can you discover the sources of hurt, disappointment, and anger that you are feeling?
- What can you do to work through those emotions and find acceptance?

Your Personal Product Development

If you are struggling with your attitude and your emotions, consider engaging a coach. A coach will challenge your thinking, help you uncover what might be holding you back, and hold you accountable for taking agreed-upon action.

Coaching isn't therapy. It is a process of self-discovery and self-generated solutions aimed at helping you achieve your full potential. Think of coaching as product development with you as the product. Aren't you worth the investment?

Face your Finances

One immediate challenge after leaving or losing a job is your personal finances. Without an income, you may be wondering:

- What happens if I can't find a job before my severance payments or unemployment run out?

- Can I file for and collect unemployment?
- How long will my savings last?
- Can I access my 401K accounts?

Before doing anything else, don't play the blame game. Whether you are blaming your company or yourself for your current circumstances, grousing about the low amount or short term of your severance payments or the cost of COBRA, stop now. Set those negative thoughts aside by working through them in your journal and start with a clean slate going forward.

The best way to deal with financial worries is to create a budget. Download a budget form (there are many household budget forms and apps available on-line – choose one that is free) and fill in the details of your current monthly income and expenses. Here are a few websites to get you started:

- [Free budget templates][4]
- [How to make a family budget][5]
- [Household budgeting worksheet][6]

---

[4] https://www.nerdwallet.com/article/finance/free-budget-spreadsheets-templates

[5] https://money.usnews.com/money/personal-finance/saving-and-budgeting/articles/how-to-make-a-family-budget

[6] https://www.kiplinger.com/kiplinger-tools/spending/t007-s001-budgeting-worksheet-a-household-budget-for-today-a/index.php

- How to create a budget in six easy steps[7]
- Podcast: Lifekit/Money/Budgets[8]

Once you have prepared your budget, sit down with your spouse or significant other and have an open discussion about how to manage your personal finances. Start by separating the needs in your budget from the wants. Needs include food, rent/mortgage, utilities, and car payments, while wants include cable, streaming, and music subscriptions, eating out, and entertainment, etc. With a record of your spending and a clarification of needs and wants, you can identify when and where cuts could be made, if or when money gets tight.

Be sure to review credit card accounts closely. It's easy to build up an extra $100+ in miscellaneous expenses each month. Don't be afraid to ask lenders for reduced or deferred payments. If you need professional assistance, make an appointment with your financial planner and/or your accountant.

This exercise puts you proactively in the driver's seat of your personal budget. Getting your financial house in order will reduce your financial worries and burdens. You will sleep more soundly and be in a better place to objectively evaluate your financial needs when that job offer comes.

---

[7] https://www.thebalance.com/how-to-make-a-budget-1289587

[8] https://podcasts.apple.com/us/podcast/be-the-master-of-your-budget/id1461493575?i=1000436702503

In addition, this exercise will help you determine the minimum salary that you can accept. This piece of data is critical when it comes to salary negotiations; particularly if you are taking a lower level job or accepting a job within a smaller organization. The more you know, the stronger your negotiating position will be.

Here are some additional ways to invite Tigger into the room:

Focus on the Positives

Where are you concentrating your energy? Winston Churchill said *"A pessimist sees the difficulty in every opportunity; an optimist sees the opportunity in every difficulty."* Are you facing opportunities or are you facing difficulties in your job search?

What draws your attention and energy? Marilee Adams, author of *Change Your Questions, Change your Life*, says, "With our questions, we make the world. Questions open our minds, our eyes, and our hearts. With our questions, we learn, connect, and create" (Adams, 2015). John Maxwell in his book, *Good Leaders ask Great Questions,* says, "Good questions inform; great questions transform."

Ask yourself, how do your current questions serve you? What are you focusing on? Difficulties or opportunities? Are your questions leading you to think more deeply, to challenge your assumptions, and to be open to innovative solutions?

Consciously focus on what you can control in your job search, not on what you can't. Ask yourself these positive questions and experience your mindset while you do:

- Start the day with this question
    - What one-step can I take today to move my search forward?
- Ask these questions every evening:
    - What went well today?
    - What could I do differently?
    - What lessons did I learn?
    - Who do I need to reach out to?

The simple change in your vocabulary from difficulties to opportunities will change the questions you are asking yourself and influence your openness and creativity in finding answers.

> ### Brian's Story
>
> One long-term job seeker, Brian, recently shared with me that his positive attitude comes from keeping in mind what he learned from the Earl Nightingale book, *The Strangest Secret*, "We become what we think about." With this as his personal mantra, Brian's attention is on where he wants to go. Even if the chips are down, Brian will find a way to get around any obstacle in his path. He doesn't hold grudges and believes that the best revenge is success.

Do you have a favorite quote or phrase that helps you remain positive? Here are a few of mine:

- "I've missed more than 9,000 shots in my career I've lost almost 300 games. 26 times I've been trusted to take the game winning shot and missed. I've failed over and over and over again in my life. And that is why I succeed." Michael Jordan
- "What lies behind you and what lies in front of you, pales in comparison to what lies inside of you." Ralph Waldo Emerson
- "The moment where you doubt you can fly, you cease forever being able to do it." Peter Pan J.M. Barrie
- "Some men see things as they are and say why—I dream things that never were and say why not." George Bernard Shaw
- "Sometimes, when things are falling apart, they may actually be falling into place." Unknown

Find a quote that resonates for you and post it on your computer, your dashboard, and/or on your mirror to reinforce the positive emotions it brings forward.

Exercise: Count Your Blessings

As job seekers, we become so caught up in our job search that we fail to recognize the blessings that are in our lives every day. Try one or more of these daily practices to become more aware of the blessings that surround you.

- Take a moment every day to look for and acknowledge the things that bring you joy.

- Make a list of what helps you feel refreshed or renewed. Maybe it's walking in the park, hugging your children, petting the cat/dog, listening to a particular song or artist, going to the movies, pursuing a hobby...etc. Anytime you are feeling overwhelmed or exhausted, pull out your list and do something for yourself.
- Pay it forward: send a thank you note – appreciating someone else takes the attention off you.
- Start a gratitude journal – Write down 3 amazing things every day. Don't think big, think of the simple gifts that surround you – a beautiful sunrise, the way the light hits the snow, the taste of that first sip of coffee or glass of wine, a simple thank you or a hug, etc. When you do this regularly, you will build your neural pathways to optimism; regardless of whether you are naturally an optimist or a pessimist.

These practices will enhance your motivation and energy; getting you through the inevitable ups and downs of your search, and providing a break from your research or networking efforts.

Banish Negativity

We all have friends or family who live in a world of negativity. You know who they are. The mere mention of their name makes you feel weary and you dread being in their presence. Their glasses are never half-full, they're always half empty. They are the Debbie or Donald Downers in our lives.

Another identifying characteristic of these friends is that they are BMWs – Bitchers, Moaners, and Whiners. Right now, it's critical to eliminate the BMWs from your life or, at least, minimize the time you spend in their presence. Their negativity can bring you down, encourage you to feel sorry for yourself, and get you stuck on the merry-go-round of negative emotions and bad attitudes. Their negativity can make you feel like your job search can't possibly have a good ending. *Woe is me…*is the mantra you hear playing in your head.

The other side of this is that **you** could be that Debbie or Donald Downer. To stay out of that dark world, appoint a negativity cop. What is a negativity cop? This is someone who will gently nudge you when you are heading down the rabbit hole of negative thoughts, emotions, and actions and challenge you to improve your outlook. Who can fill this important role? Find a caring person who is close to you such as a friend, spouse, or job search partner.

Surround Yourself with Support

Another option for maintaining a positive attitude is to join a job search group. What is a job search group? Simply put, it's a support group for job seekers in transition or those wishing to change careers. It's a place to get your questions answered and to share your challenges, obstacles, and successes with other job seekers.

If it's been a long time since you were in the job market, you'll need to learn how to:

- market yourself in a whole new way
- incorporate social media into your search

- find "hidden" positions
- get advice, information and referrals
- network effectively

Job search groups provide a multitude of services such as LinkedIn photos, interview practice, resume reviews, and networking tips. Some groups bring in speakers on topics related to transition and job search success while others focus on discussion and problem solving related to job search obstacles. The tools, resources, techniques, and networking opportunities offered will help you maximize your job search efforts

The leaders of these groups are often business owners, retired executives and HR leaders who want to give back by helping others. They offer their expertise, their network connections, and their listening ears.

To find job search groups in your area of the country, check Google, Meetup,[9] your local library, and nearby houses of worship for job search support or job seeker groups. No groups in your area? Consider starting one with the step-by-step guide in this article: "How to Create a Job Search Support Group"[10]

In a job search group, you will surround yourself with the support, encouragement, and inspiration of other job seekers. Sharing time with

---

[9] https://www.meetup.com/

[10] https://www.forbes.com/sites/nextavenue/2018/01/07/how-to-create-a-job-search-support-group/#5060385e3d0c

other job seekers can help you get your job search started, maintain your momentum, and accelerate your success. You will feel more productive and ramp up your skills in the search process.

> ### Job Search Groups in Northeast Ohio
>
> For those of you who live or work in Northeast Ohio, these job search support groups are ready to help you focus and energize your search:
>
> - <u>Hudson Job Search</u>[11] – Holds seminars on critical job search & career topics at no charge.
> - <u>North Canton Executive Networking Group</u>[12] – Meetings feature speakers on job search topics. Leadership team provides resume review, interview practice, and much more.
> - <u>Northcoast Job Seekers</u>[13] – Meetings alternate networking with professional speakers.
> - <u>Summit Networking Group</u>[14] – Exclusively for senior managers and above, SNG meets twice monthly and focuses on making connections and offers problem solving of common job search obstacles.

---

[11] https://hudsonjobsearch.org/

[12] https://nceng.weebly.com/

[13] https://www.northcoastjobseekers.org/

[14] mailto:marsha@consultmef.com

> In addition, the State of Ohio offers free online career counseling through Ohio Means Jobs[15] (OMJ). OMJ connects businesses to job seekers and provides career services to all Ohioans.

Failure Leads to Success

Just like riding a bike, you learn something every time you fall down. Failure gives us feedback, so embrace it! During your job search, each of these events might feel like a personal failure:

- You got no response to your applications.
- You didn't get past the phone screen.
- You weren't selected for a 2nd interview.
- The offer didn't match your expectations.
- You didn't get an offer—again.

Get back up, brush yourself off, and use what you have learned to be better prepared for the next opportunity that comes your way.

The only path to success is through failure. Anyone who is successful, has failed their way to the top. The weekly NPR show and podcast *How I Built This*[16] is filled with stories of failure on the path to success. For

---

[15] https://jobseeker.ohiomeansjobs.monster.com/
[16] https://www.npr.org/podcasts/510313/how-i-built-this

inspiration, listen to an episode or two of *How I Built This*.

If you aren't failing, maybe you are not aiming at your full potential. Take a lesson from Sarah Robb O'Hagan, CEO of EXOS and author of *Extreme You*. I became acquainted with Sarah when I was researching the benefits of failure. I listened to the episode "*Bouncing Back From Rejection*"[17] on Adam Grant's Work/Life Podcast. In that interview, Sarah talks about her job history, which is littered with what she refers to as "Epic Failures." Through these failures, Sarah learned several key lessons about the role of blame in failure.

- Initially, in our effort to protect ourselves, we direct the blame outward. We think: *It's not me, it's you*!
- The next stage in the blame game is looking inward, blaming ourselves: *It's not you, it's really me!*
- As we move toward acceptance, we realize that the cause of the failure is shared. There was a mismatch in the relationship: *It's us!*

If you have Epic Failures in your job history, consider highlighting them in your LinkedIn profile as Sarah O'Hagan does in hers.[18]

Exercise: Is Fear Holding You Back?

Is fear holding you back from failing? If so, face your fears, and let them

---

[17] https://podcasts.apple.com/us/podcast/bouncing-back-from-rejection/id1346314086?i=1000435037507

[18] https://www.linkedin.com/in/sarah-robb-o-hagan-249130/

go. Below you'll find a chart with "action" and "inaction" on the x-axis and "best" and "worst" on the y-axis. The questions in the chart below will reveal the outcomes of facing your fears. By answering these four simple questions, you'll be poised for action, being more confident and comfortable in making a decision to move forward. In addition, you will understand the risks and the rewards of taking action.

	ACTION	INACTION
BEST	What's the best thing that can happen if I do this thing?	What's the best thing that can happen if I don't do this thing?
WORST	What's the worst thing that can happen if I do this thing?	What's the worst thing that can happen if I don't do this thing?

Samantha's Story

With two job offers on the table, Samantha was afraid to make a decision. To get the evaluation process moving forward we worked through the fear matrix starting with *What's the best that can happen if I don't accept this offer?* She would enjoy an increase in pay as her current company matched the offers on the table, but with no opportunity for additional pay increases or advancement within that organization. The next question was *What's the worst thing that can happen if I don't take this offer?* Status quo with no control over travel requirements. *What's the worst thing that can happen if I do accept this offer?* If changing companies didn't work out for Samantha, she was in a high demand field and another company would snap her up as soon as she became

> available. *What's the best thing that can happen if I accept this offer?* New opportunities, new challenges and less travel which were critical to Samantha who had 3 school age children at home. In the end, this process surfaced one fear behind Samantha's reluctance to make a decision. We strategized a follow-up question to ask and with that answer, Samantha confidently accepted the job offer.

Take a Vacation

I'm giving you permission to take time off or take a vacation during your job search. Just like training for a marathon, give yourself time-off to prevent mental and emotional burnout. The benefit is renewed energy and motivation when you return. Take a day, a weekend, or a week off from your search. Give yourself permission to:

- Sneak out to a movie or binge watch a show
- Take an afternoon off to play golf
- Go for a walk, a hike or a bike ride
- Phone a friend
- Go to the pool

Think of your vacation as a time for an attitude adjustment. If you are angry, frustrated, or anxious because you haven't taken a break from your search, those emotions will come through loud and clear to your family and friends, and, most importantly, your contacts. Remember, your attitude flaunts itself during your phone calls, meetings, and interviews.

As a vacation bonus, you don't know whom you will meet while you are off and those chance meetings can help you connect to your next opportunity.

> *"Do the thing you are afraid to do and the death of fear is certain."*
>
> —Ralph Waldo Emerson

CHAPTER 3
STAND OUT:
Increase Your Value

"Learning is not attained by chance, it must be sought for with ardor and attended to with diligence."

—Abigail Adams

"Never stop learning"—that's the mantra of every lifelong learner and job seeker. Lifelong learners seek new information, follow the latest research, and try the next new thing. As a job seeker who wants to demonstrate value to prospective employers, you work to fill gaps in your skill set, research your industry and market, and eliminate your challenges.

As the length of your job search grows, you will begin to think about the expanding time gap between jobs on your resume. How will you answer the likely questions from prospective employers about that employment gap including:

- What have you been doing in the interim?
- How have you maintained and updated your skills?

One way to ensure that you have a solid answer to these questions is to continue your education. There are many free or inexpensive learning and assessment options that will extend your knowledge base, increase your employability, and provide you with conversation starters for interviews.

Establish Your Learning Goals

Your learning goals can be found in the answers to these questions:

- What knowledge, skills, or abilities would enhance my expertise?
- How can I stay current in my field of expertise and in my industry?
- If I am changing careers or changing industries, what certifications or processes do I need to research, learn, and understand?
- What behaviors have held me back in prior positions and how can I learn to respond differently?

Armed with the answers to these questions, you can establish your learning goals and begin to fill any gaps in your expertise or competencies. Using the goal setting and action planning worksheet in Chapter 4, fill in your goals, taking into consideration your timeline for completion as well as the obstacles you may face and the support you may need. Once you have your goals established, go through the list of learning options, and decide which option would best support your learning needs and your learning style.

Learning Options

There are a range of learning options available that are low-priced or free. Let's start with online learning.

- MOOCs (massive open online communities) such as EdX,[19] Coursera,[20] and FutureLearn[21] offer a range of courses from top tier colleges and universities including MIT, Case Western Reserve, and the London School of Economics to name a few. Their online course catalogs offer a full array of subjects and are free to anyone who wants to audit the courses. You have full access to all learning resources, articles, videos, and workbooks. *Note: If you want to get credit for the work completed or obtain a certification, you will be required to pay a relatively modest fee.*

- LinkedIn Learning[22] offers classes to build your skillset. If you are a LinkedIn Premium member, their courses are free. If not, you can subscribe on a monthly basis. There is no per course fee option. Check with your local library to see if they have a subscription, which would make Lynda free to you.

- Udemy[23] is a pay-by-course learning provider. Their content comes from a variety of instructors so watch the previews and choose carefully. The average cost of a course is $12 making this a reasonable option if you are just interested in one or two courses or topics. Udemy offers over 65,000 courses so they have a wide variety of content but they don't offer any certifications.

---

[19] https://www.edx.org/

[20] https://www.coursera.org/

[21] https://www.futurelearn.com/

[22] https://www.linkedin.com/learning

[23] https://www.udemy.com/

Other learning resources to consider include:

- Books – study a book about leadership, read the biography of a leader you admire, or pick up a classic like Napoleon Hill's *Think & Grow Rich*, Malcolm Gladwell's *Outliers* or Stephen Covey's *7 Habits of Highly Effective People*. See Appendix A for book recommendations from the author.
- Magazines – read the latest issues of *Forbes*, *Harvard Business Review*, or the *Wall Street Journal*.
- Podcasts – download and listen to podcasts on business, psychology, entrepreneurship, or leadership.
- TED Talks[24] – watch TED Talks on a variety of topics. If you've never watched a TED Talk, start with the 25 most popular to spur your thinking and engagement.
- LinkedIn – read blog posts or articles from thought leaders in your industry.
- Google Alerts – set up Google Alerts on relevant industry topics, then post those articles along with your comments on LinkedIn.

Your learning will enable you to stay current on industry trends and changes and to have conversation starters for interviews and networking meetings. You can use the articles from Google Alerts to share your thoughts, start a discussion on LinkedIn, or share an article directly with your contacts who might benefit from the information. This is another

---

[24] https://www.ted.com/talks

way to remain top of mind with your network and to demonstrate the value you bring to the workplace.

Comfort with Video & Screen Presence

Now is the time to get comfortable with video meeting technology and appearing on camera. If you don't have one yet, get a Zoom account (it's free).

To work on your screen presence, open a solo Zoom by clicking on Host a Meeting. Carry your laptop, cellphone or tablet around the house to find the best background and lighting. You may need to improve your equipment setup to get the best visuals — for example, be sure your camera isn't aimed at the ceiling or under your chin. Use indirect rather than overhead lighting and be careful with sunlight from windows. It can wash out your image or fill your screen with glare. Also, if you wear glasses, try to make sure the light isn't reflecting so that it hides your eyes or is too distracting.

To stay focused on the camera, put a smiley face around the camera using a sticky note. Then you'll know where to look to create "eye contact" with your interviewers. Remember, if you are focusing on their pictures on the screen, you will not be looking directly at them.

Be sure that your name shows on your image. To correct your name:

- click on participant
- find your name
- click on more and then rename

Add a professional picture to your Zoom site in your profile. When you are entering a meeting, before your video comes on, you will present a professional image.

Test your audio by opening a meeting with a friend or your spouse to check your reception and volume. You can use your computer's microphone or you can use a Bluetooth headset. At some point, a higher quality microphone (like a Blue Yeti) on a boom arm might be a modest, but worthwhile investment.

Carefully consider your appearance. What are you wearing to your job search group meetings, screening calls, networking meetings, and interviews? If you answered pajamas, sweat pants, or shorts, think again. Consider dressing the part for the job you are seeking. Casual dress may give you permission to be casual in your language and your attitude. Keeping up a professional appearance will show that you mean business and that you respect yourself and those who are making time to meet with you.

Practice, practice, practice. You need to get used to seeing yourself on screen and displaying stronger emotion and using larger gestures as you speak. Open a Zoom meeting with a friend or job search buddy and practice answering likely interview questions. Get comfortable with this technology. It is here to stay!

> **Laurie's story**
>
> Laurie, a long-term job seeker, who gets satisfaction from helping other people, recognized early in the Covid-19 pandemic that Zoom would become the platform of choice for groups and organizations to replace in-person gatherings. Laurie quickly set out to learn as much as she could about this new technology and made herself a resource for senior centers, job search groups, and associations. Laurie teaches classes to both groups and individuals and offers her skills as facilitator and group leader across the community. As she says, "these are skills that will benefit me down the line and enable me to help other people connect." What expertise do you have that can help others? What topics or technologies do you want to become expert in?

Assess Yourself

If you haven't taken the opportunity to complete assessments of your work behaviors and/or personal preferences, now is a great time to do that. In addition to gaining an understanding of what makes you tick and how you come across in the workplace, you can use what you learn in responding to interview questions.

The assessments listed below are available at minimal cost. (Both *StrengthsFinder 2.0* and *Emotional Intelligence 2.0* are books that are readily available through Amazon and other online book retailers). Although there are free versions online of both the DiSC assessment and Myers Briggs Type Indicator, my strong recommendation is to work with a personal development or leadership coach to gain their insight and interpretation of your assessment results. The small investment will be well worthwhile.

StrengthsFinder 2.0[25] by Tom Rath – Starting with an online assessment, you will:

- Identify your top 5 strengths
- Discover what you naturally do best
- Learn to maximize your talents
- Direct your strengths development efforts and limit overuse of your strengths

What does it mean to work to your strengths? The day flies by, you are fully engaged working at your peak level of performance. When you are doing work that isn't one of your strengths, you might feel like you are swimming through sand.

As a bonus, you can refer to your top five strengths in your interviews when potential employers pose questions such as tell me about yourself. Once you know your strengths, you can find ways to weave them into your resume, your marketing plan, and your interview stories.

You can also use your strengths as an evaluation tool as you review the offers you receive. Consider how much of your time in the new job will

---

[25] https://www.amazon.com/StrengthsFinder-2-0-Tom-Rath/dp/159562015X/ref=sr_1_1?crid=2YY0H748HQFVB&dchild=1&keywords=strengthsfinder+2.0+with+access+code&qid=1598037071&sprefix=strengthsfinder%2Caps%2C1173&sr=8-1

be devoted to work that brings out your best self—work that energizes and strengthens you.

Many employers are familiar with StrengthsFinder and some teams use strengths to influence the distribution of work tasks.

Emotional Intelligence 2.0[26] by Travis Bradberry & Jean Greaves. The book includes a key to an online assessment, which can be taken twice to measure your learning progress. Working through EI 2.0 will help you:

- Understand the impact of emotional intelligence
- Evaluate your emotional intelligence scores
- Discover how to improve your emotional intelligence competencies through specific behavioral changes

Daniel Goleman is considered the father of Emotional Intelligence and his book *Emotional Intelligence* was groundbreaking when it was published in 2001. *Emotional Intelligence 2.0* is a good starting point for learning how your behaviors impact your success in the workplace.

DiSC profiles help you increase your self-knowledge based on your workplace behaviors. Your report will highlight your response to conflict, your motivations, your stressors, and your problem-solving style. One of the greatest benefits to DiSC is understanding how to

---

[26] https://www.amazon.com/Emotional-Intelligence-2-0-Travis-Bradberry/dp/0974320625/ref=sr_1_3?crid=H1HAW01K94YR&dchild=1&keywords=emotional+intelligence+2.0&qid=1598037130&sprefix=emotiona%2Caps%2C219&sr=8-3

improve interactions with others to achieve higher workplace satisfaction and results.

<u>Myers Briggs Type Indicator</u> (MBTI) assessments help you navigate the world through the lenses of your personal preferences which are hard-wired like right or left-handedness. The MBTI assessment provides you with a profile indicating your hard-wired preferences in these four areas:

- Energy Sources: Where do you get your energy, from other people or from solitude?
- Information: Do you accept the basic information you take in or do you interpret that information and add meaning?
- Decisions: When making decisions, do you first consider logic and consistency or people and special circumstances?
- Structure: Is your life planned out and scheduled or more free form and spontaneous?

Through the MBTI assessment, you will enhance your own self-awareness and self-management and have a better understanding of those with whom you work and interact every day.

Define Your Values

How will you know if you fit culturally into a new organization? Start by defining your core own values. What do you care about? What makes you feel fulfilled? What makes you angry? What disappoints you? The answers to these questions are a good starting point for recognizing your personal values.

Once you have a list of your personal values, the next step is to match those to the organization's values. You can discover the stated values of the organization by reviewing their website. Then seek validation by talking to both current and former employees. As Peter Drucker said, *"Culture eats strategy for breakfast."* In other words, despite the stated vision, mission, and values of the organization, the real organizational culture is defined by exhibited behaviors. If you don't fit in culturally, then you won't be happy and your employment will be short-term.

<u>**Exercise: Your Core Values**</u> Set aside 10 minutes and go through the 5 simple steps in this exercise to discover your core values. *Grab a pen and piece of paper and go!*

1. Determine your core values. As you read through the list below, simply circle the words that feel like a core value to you personally. Do not overthink your choices. Don't limit yourself to this list; if you think of a value that is not on the list, write it down.

Abundance	Dignity	Inclusiveness	Relationships
Accountability	Diligence	Independence	Responsibility
Acceptance	Diplomacy	Influence	Resourcefulness
Accuracy	Discretion	Ingenuity	Responsiveness
Achievement	Dynamism	Innovation	Restraint
Adventure	Elegance	Inspiration	Rigor
Altruism	Efficiency	Integrity	Risk Taking
Ambition	Empathy	Intelligence	Security

Appreciation	Enthusiasm	Intuition	Self-Control
Authenticity	Enjoyment	Joy	Selflessness
Authority	Equality	Justice	Self-Reliance
Autonomy	Excellence	Kindness	Serenity
Balance	Excitement	Knowledge	Service
Beauty	Expertise	Leadership	Simplicity
Boldness	Fairness	Learning	Social
Bravery	Faith	Love	Spirituality
Calmness	Flexibility	Loyalty	Spontaneity
Caring	Forgiveness	Mastery	Stability
Celebration	Freedom	Mindfulness	Status
Challenge	Fun	Mutual Respect	Success
Cheerfulness	Generosity	Openness	Teamwork
Citizenship	Grace	Optimism	Thankfulness
Community	Gratitude	Passion	Thoughtfulness
Compassion	Growth	Peace	Trustworthiness
Competence	Happiness	Perseverance	Understanding
Contentment	Harmony	Playfulness	Uniqueness
Contribution	Health	Pleasure	Usefulness
Control	Helping	Poise	Versatility
Cooperation	Honesty	Popularity	Vision
Courtesy	Hope	Practicality	Warmth
Creativity	Honor	Prudence	Wealth
Curiosity	Humility	Purpose	Well-being
Determination	Humor	Recognition	Wisdom
Development	Impact	Reputation	Zest

2. Group similar values together. Using the list you just created, group the values in a way that makes sense to you. Create a maximum of five groupings. If you have more than five groupings, drop the least important grouping(s).

Abundance	Acceptance	Appreciation	Balance	Playfulness
Growth	Compassion	Contribution	Health	Fun
Wealth	Inclusiveness	Thankfulness	Development	Happiness
Security	Intuition	Caring	Spirituality	Humor
Freedom	Kindness	Mindfulness	Well-being	Inspiration
Flexibility	Love			Joy
Peace	Impact			Optimism

3. Choose one word from each group that represents the label for the entire group. Do not overthink your labels — there are no right or wrong answers. You are defining the answer that is right for you.

Freedom	Impact	Mindfulness	Well-being	Happiness

4. Add a verb to each value label so you can see what it looks like as an actionable core value. For example:

- Live in **freedom**.
- Seek opportunities to make an **impact**.
- Act with **mindfulness**.
- Promote **well-being**.

- Multiply **happiness**.

This will guide you in the actions you need to take to feel like you are truly living your values.

5. Finally, post your core values. Write your core values in order of priority in your planner, so they are available as an easy reference when you are faced with decisions. Put them on a sticky note on the edge of your computer screen or make a background with them on it for your cell phone. Consider posting your values on your bathroom mirror as a daily reminder. Keep a copy on your dashboard.

Valerie's Story

My client, Valerie, shared that her previous job lasted only 18 months. She attributes her short tenure to a mismatch in values and culture. As a result, Valerie is being much more cautious and resourceful in discovering and validating organizational values and culture before she accepts her next opportunity. I'm happy to report that despite several setbacks and a lengthy 15-month search, Valerie landed a job with an organization that shares her values and appears to be a good fit.

"The illiterate of the 21st century will not be those who cannot read and write, but those who cannot learn, unlearn, and relearn."

—Alvin Toffler

Chapter 4
BUILD MOMENTUM:
Action brings success

"Setting goals is the first step in turning the invisible into the visible."

—Tony Robbins

Congratulations! You made it! Now that you've fine-tuned your self-care, adjusted your attitude and established a learning program, it's time to take action.

Job seekers who miss their daily dose of problem-solving and goal-achievement will find comfort in this chapter. The actions recommended here put you immediately back in work mode creating goals for your job search (goal setting), finding ways to overcome adversity (maintaining focus and forward momentum), getting the support and help you need (building a team), and answering the question about full-time vs. part-time work (decision-making). Don't hesitate one moment longer, dig in and get started!

Set Goals & Celebrate Wins

To hold yourself accountable for making progress, consider setting daily, weekly, or monthly goals for your job search. You could set goals for:

- Updating your resume
- Creating a marketing plan
- Researching industries or specific organizations
- Following up on leads and/or contacts
- Attending networking meetings or events
- Identifying associations or business groups to visit
- Meeting with a career counselor, job coach, or resume writer
- Joining a job search support group
- Developing your interview stories
- Practicing interview skills
- Setting up Google Alerts related to your industry
- Enrolling in online learning class

Having goals with specific tasks to complete will help you minimize and/or eliminate procrastination. Craft your goals as SMART goals.

SMART goals are:

Specific – Goals should be clear and concrete, and precisely describe the desired outcome. If a goal is not specific, it won't be measurable. You may also find it difficult to determine whether the goal is realistic and achievable.

Measurable – Goals must be measurable. A measurable goal is one that has definite criteria for its success. A good rule for determining a goal's measurability is to answer the question, how will I know whether the goal has been accomplished?

Achievable – Goals need to be achievable. You should be able to attain your goals by exerting some effort/stretching.

Realistic – Goals must be realistic. Knowing what your abilities and time commitments are will help you determine whether a goal is realistic.

Time bound – Goals should be time bound, with definite starting points, durations, and ending points. In other words, think about time lines and deadlines when setting goals. These factors will also help you measure the outcome of a goal.

Once your goals are defined, the next step is to break your goals into smaller tasks to make them more manageable. Take into account the obstacles you may encounter along the way and consider the help and support you may need. Having a list of people you can rely on will help you maintain forward momentum.

Once you have finished planning your goals, you can create structure for yourself. Set specific office hours for your search and provide space in your schedule for exercise, family time, as well as your outside interests.

Celebrate your wins as you complete tasks and achieve your goals. Creating celebrations for your accomplishments provides motivation to keep your search on track. Celebrations can be as simple as a cup of coffee, a glass of wine, a walk around the block, playing with your dog or cat or your children, reading a book, or watching an episode of your favorite TV show. Select celebrations that motivate you and keep moving you forward.

Several job seekers shared with me that staying on a schedule, getting up at the same time every day, taking the search one day at a time, and filling up their calendars with search related tasks were all key to staying centered and energized.

Here is a goal-setting worksheet that you can use as a template to start your planning:

GOAL SETTING AND ACTION PLANNING WORKSHEET

Goal	
Action Steps (tasks)	**Target Date**
Obstacle(s)	**How to overcome them**
Support	**Assistance this person could provide**

Procrastination

When it comes to setting goals and taking action, I would be remiss if I didn't include some guidance on eliminating or, at least, reducing procrastination. All of us find ways to procrastinate or delay the tasks that we know can move us forward.

Often the causes of procrastination are emotional. If you look at the tasks you are putting off, you will likely notice that you are saying to yourself that you don't want to get this wrong, that you don't know how to get started, that you aren't up to the task, or similar negative thoughts. This negativity drives our self-esteem down and increases our reluctance to get the task started. Show yourself some compassion by not judging your work before you get started. Like brainstorming, make a rule not to criticize your work while you are in the creative phase.

Recognize that we all have a "should-self" and a "want-self." The want-self demands instant gratification while the should-self looks to longer-term interest. Our should-self has productive tasks to be completed while our want-self has stuff that we like to do and excel at like binge watching our favorite show, getting lost in social media, or playing video games. In order to delay the gratification of our want-self, it might be necessary to sign off of social media, turn off our cell phones, or make binge watching a reward for completing one or more of our *should* tasks. Another strategy is to create a "To Don't" list of activities to avoid while working.

Institute a 3/1 rule

For every one negative action that happens during your job search, take three positive actions. Any three actions that move your search forward will do. Here are a few suggestions:

- reach out to a networking contact by phone or email
- send a thank-you note
- schedule a networking meeting
- search LinkedIn for a connection
- phone a friend for support

You get the idea. Any activity that keeps you focused positively in your search counts as one of your three actions. Use this 3/1 rule to maintain forward momentum, even in those situations when you are feeling defeated or discouraged.

Keep in mind that every "no" you hear gets you closer to the "yes" you are seeking.

Partner Up!

Do you have a job search buddy or an accountability partner?

What's a job search buddy? Someone who is actively engaged in their own job search and is willing to share their successes, failures, and lessons learned. You can serve as each other's interview partner, hold each other accountable for reaching your goals, and have someone to talk to about the ups and downs of the search process. Think of your job search buddy as someone with whom you can commiserate and/or celebrate.

You and your job search buddy do not have to be in the same professional field. When I was in search mode, my buddy was a former colleague whose expertise was in supply chains while mine was in organizational development. We attended job search and networking meetings together, shared feedback on resumes and cover letters, made introductions, and provided emotional support.

What's an accountability partner? Simply stated, an accountability partner holds you responsible for doing what you said you will do. During your job search an accountability partner could be your job search buddy, a friend, or career coach.

What's the value of having an accountability partner? The Association for Training & Development (ATD) recently published a study that showed the impact of having an accountability partner on the likelihood of reaching your goals.

- If you simply have an idea or goal, like a New Year's resolution, your success rate will be 10-25%.
- Once you develop a timeline and are clear on how you are going to get there, your success rate will move up to 50%-50%.
- If you tell someone about your goal, this increases your potential of success to 65%
- When you commit to an accountability partner, and know that

someone will be checking on your progress, your success will skyrocket to 95%.

Run, don't walk, to find an accountability partner and increase your prospects for a successful search.

Ask for & Accept Help

Asking for and accepting help is one of the hardest things for human beings to do, especially for job seekers whose careers have been marked by success. We tend to "over-rely on self-reliance" and are extremely reluctant to admit that we even need help. Compounding that reluctance, we want to be seen as independent, competent, and resourceful.

While asking for help can be humbling, it can also be an extremely rewarding part of the job search process. By asking for help you will develop more and deeper relationships. Rather than looking down on you, your friends, family, and colleagues will recognize your bravery and your gumption. They will reward your efforts (your "ask") by fulfilling your requests.

In his book, *All You Have to Do Is Ask*,[27] Wayne Baker shares, based on research from Wharton and Harvard, that if you make a rational, reasonable request, you are viewed as more competent, not less. This

---

[27] https://www.amazon.com/All-You-Have-Ask-Important/dp/1984825925/ref=tmm_hrd_swatch_0?_encoding=UTF8&qid=1598037644&sr=8-1

same study revealed that we often underestimate other people's willingness and ability to help. We are wired to help others, not ask for help for ourselves.

The critical part of asking for help is being specific in your ask. Don't just ask for general assistance — let the other party know exactly what you need, when you need it, and how they can support you. For example:

- an interview practice partner
- an introduction to a particular person
- information about the company's hiring practices or culture
- feedback on your elevator pitch

Baker suggests using the acronym SMART when making your request.

- S stands for specific – provide details of the ask
- M is for meaningful – explain why is this ask is important
- A equals action – be specific about what action needs to be taken
- R stands for real or realistic – this is a task that supports a larger goal
- T is for time-bound – identify when this is required

Be direct in your ask. Start by simply asking, "Can you give me some advice?" Then be vulnerable and lead with what you can't do. For example, "I'm struggling to find the right words for my elevator pitch and I have no idea how to improve it." Using simple language, being straightforward and humble will get the answer you are hoping for.

Asking for advice makes those you ask feel important and will elevate others' opinion of you. If you do get a no, reach out to someone else, remember none of us can say yes to every ask. Don't hesitate to ask a "dormant" connection. Often those individuals who with whom we haven't connected have new insights to share and are delighted to hear from us.

Don't forget to say "thank you," show your gratitude, and offer something of value to those who come to your aid. Whenever you can show the value that you bring, you will deepen your relationships and remain top of mind.

Give Back

Job seekers get so consumed with themselves and their job search, but it is good to take time away to help others. By giving, you will receive more in return. Serving others brings a release of endorphins (think "runner's high"), which increases happiness and energy while reducing anxiety and depression.

Volunteering can benefit your job search in other ways, as well. I know one job seeker who was leading a project for the non-profit where he was a board member. The board was so impressed by his work that they created a full-time role for this job seeker.

While the work that you are doing for a non-profit may not lead to a direct job offer, you don't know with who you may be working and how meeting new people on the board or the staff might expand your network. Plus, there is always something to learn from working with another organization. You will gain much more than you give when you open yourself up to volunteer work. Best of all, giving to others provides us with the gift of positivity and personal fulfillment.

Consider Contract Work

Your job search is centered on full-time employment but you just got an offer for contract work that is right up your alley. Now, what? What factors do you need to consider? How is part-time or contract work viewed in an interview? Will a part-time or contract job derail your search?

The benefits of contract or project work are significant, starting with reducing or diminishing gaps in your employment record and filling your resume with additional accomplishments. Being out of the workplace makes you feel stale and the opportunity to jump back in and stretch those "muscles" will have the benefit of keeping your skills fresh. If you are trying to change industries or career paths, a part-time or contract job will provide a "test" period to prove your skills to a potential employer. The monies you make can fill the income gap while you continue to pursue full-time employment. Increasing your network connections is an added benefit.

While there is no guarantee, part-time project or contract work can result in a job offer or lead to a career decision. During my job search, I was approached by a non-profit organization to sit in on a job interview for a temporary worker. In a discussion with the board members after the interview, I suggested that they consider performing a process review before jumping into hiring. As a result, I was engaged for a process improvement project, which went well beyond the original scope adding software and database replacement as well as implementation. This project was the start for my consulting and coaching practice.

The biggest potential drawback or challenge to working part-time is balancing between work and your job search. How will you maintain momentum and continue your job search while working? Can you take time off to attend job search groups or to schedule phone or in-person interviews? Will you take a break from your search and concentrate on this assignment to make a good impression on your new employer? Your challenge is to think through each of these questions as you consider the offer on the table.

If you make the decision to accept a part-time or contract job, you will want to get counsel concerning the need for:

- Setting up an LLC or other legal structure — may require working with an attorney
- Purchasing commercial liability insurance
- Creating a fee structure
- Developing contract documents
- Establishing a business banking relationship

The decision to work during a job search is as individual as every job seeker. Understanding the pros and cons will help you make an informed decision that is right for you and your circumstances.

Other Part-time Work

A recent LinkedIn story that went viral was about someone who lost a corporate job and started doing odd jobs in the neighborhood (painting, mowing lawns, fixing things, etc.) to support his family. He was ridiculed by former colleagues who thought this work was beneath him. This job seeker quickly got referrals and expanded to more than compensate for his lost income. The comments on this post were overwhelmingly positive, filled with stories of resilience and advice on reevaluating a career direction and expectations. Recruiters talked about the learning, dedication and drive exhibited by job seekers who take on work outside of their area of expertise. The moral of this story is to do what works for you and disregard the naysayers. Follow your heart and your gut and you won't be lead astray.

"Whatever you think you can do or believe you can do, begin it. Action has magic, grace, and power in it."

—Johann Wolfgang Von Goethe

SUMMARY

Job Search Mastery was written to provide the guidance, encouragement, and inspiration to job seekers that is missing from other job search books. The strategies, tips, and exercises in Chapters 1-4 are aimed to eliminate sleepless nights of worry and despair caused by:

- pressures from self, family, and finances
- the length of the job search
- the challenge of maintaining focus and motivation
- wavering self-confidence

Chapter 1 addressed self-care from head to toe, evaluating your emotional and physical health in order to unleash your best self. Chapter 2 increased your understating of mental fitness, attitude, and the influence of self and others on our mindset. Chapter 3 challenged you to create a learning plan to expand your expertise and keep your skills and knowledge current. Chapter 4 set you up to maintain forward momentum through goal setting, overcoming negative actions, identifying sources of support, and walking through the pros and cons of contract work.

By the end of *Job Search Mastery*, you are now bringing your best self to every meeting and interview, along with enhanced skills and industry expertise and a more optimistic attitude. With a solid base of support behind you and strong forward momentum, may your journey to a new job be a smooth ride.

APPENDIX A
RECOMMENDED BOOKS

Clients often ask me what books I recommend. As an avid reader and lifelong learner, I've always got a book in my hand. Here are some of my favorite books broken into two categories: leading others and leading yourself. These categories stem from my personal belief that each of us, regardless of job title, are leaders.

Leading Others

The Anatomy of Peace[28] by The Arbinger Institute – This book focuses on how to manage conflict. Conflict at home, in the workplace, and in the community all stem from the same root cause. Individually and collectively, we choose war over peace. *The Anatomy of Peace* teaches us how to break that cycle of conflict and find lasting peace. The book is told in parable style following a group of parents on their way to drop their troubled children off at a camp to be fixed. The discussion that ensues touches every parent and impacts every relationship in their lives, personal as well as professional.

---

[28] https://www.amazon.com/Anatomy-Peace-Resolving-Heart-Conflict-dp-1523089822/dp/1523089822/ref=dp_ob_title_bk

The Checklist Manifesto[29] by Atul Gawande – Dr. Gawande, a surgeon, shows us how creating and using checklists can decrease error rates and create improvements in businesses of all kinds. An excellent guide for error proofing your workplace.

Leadership Step by Step[30] by Joshua Spodek – Spodek's formula for leadership training is one part art (improv, acting, sports, dance) and one part leadership theory. The book is divided into 4 sections: Understanding Yourself, Leading Yourself, Understanding Others, and Leading Others. To get the most out of this book, take the time to read and implement each chapter by completing the exercises, considering the reflection questions and the post-exercise before moving on to the next chapter. Your time will be well spent.

Radical Candor[31] by Kim Scott – Scott, a former Google Executive and a leader in her own company, shares her hard-learned lessons on what not to do. This book is about creating a culture of radical candor where expectations are clear and feedback is given with directness and honesty, creating a win-win for the individual, the team, the leader, and the

---

[29] https://www.amazon.com/Checklist-Manifesto-How-Things-Right/dp/0312430000/ref=sr_1_1?crid=1LE7EJUAKLWTG&dchild=1&keywords=checklist+manifesto&qid=1605559088&s=books&sprefix=checklist+%2Cstripbooks%2C206&sr=1-1

[30] https://www.amazon.com/Leadership-Step-Become-Person-Others-ebook/dp/B01HUER0ZQ/ref=sr_1_3?dchild=1&keywords=Leadership+step+by+step&qid=1605559225&s=books&sr=1-3

[31] https://www.amazon.com/Radical-Candor-Revised-Kim-Scott/dp/1250258405/ref=sr_1_2?dchild=1&keywords=Radical+Candor&qid=1605559331&s=books&sr=1-2

organization. Scott's advice is: don't hold back, be brutally honest, and tell it like it is. She illustrates how holding back does no one any good, but is a disservice to the employee, his/her co-workers, the team, and to you as his/her manager or supervisor.

<u>Rising Strong</u>[32] by Brene Brown – Being brave and vulnerable on our way to creativity, innovation and joy, leads to inevitable failures along the way. In *Rising Strong*, Brown takes us through the emotional journey from failure to success. Along the way, we learn to open ourselves to our emotions and our feelings, challenge our stories to find new realities, and get back up again. This renewal process gets us in touch with who we are.

<u>Start with Why</u>[33] by Simon Sinek – Sinek expands and deepens the message of his TED video about the importance of understanding why we do what we do. This book teaches us how the concept of the Golden Circle (What, How, Why) applies to the way inspirational leaders think, act, and communicate.

---

[32] https://www.amazon.com/Rising-Strong-Ability-Transforms-Parent/dp/081298580X/ref=sr_1_2?crid=45JQCEM5N79Y&dchild=1&keywords=rising+strong+by+brene+brown&qid=1605559413&s=books&sprefix=rising+strong%2Cstripbooks%2C248&sr=1-2

[33] https://www.amazon.com/Start-Why-Leaders-Inspire-Everyone/dp/1591846447/ref=tmm_pap_swatch_0?_encoding=UTF8&qid=1598800805&sr=8-1

Leading Yourself

All You Have to Do is Ask[34] by Wayne Baker – Asking for help is one of the hardest things that we do in life. Most people thrive on helping others but are reluctant to ask for help for themselves. Baker details a simple process to master this critical personal and professional skill.

Change Your Questions, Change Your Life[35] by Marilee Adams – Adams challenges us to reframe our questions and shift our thinking to move from naming and blaming to creating positive outcomes. She takes us out of our fight or flight mentality into opening our hearts and minds to new possibilities.

Emotional Intelligence 2.0[36] by Travis Bradberry and Jean Greaves - *EI 2.0* is an excellent introduction to the concept of Emotional Intelligence. The first 50 pages provide the science behind Emotional Intelligence (EQ), explains how EQ impacts our personal and professional success, and gives examples of both high and low EQ scores. The beauty of this book is access to an online personal,

---

[34] https://www.amazon.com/s?k=All+You+Have+to+Do+Is+Ask%3A+How+to+master+the+most+important+skill+for+success&i=stripbooks&ref=nb_sb_noss

[35] https://www.amazon.com/Change-Your-Questions-Life-Leadership/dp/162656633X/ref=sr_1_1?dchild=1&keywords=change+your+questions+change+your+life+marilee+adams&qid=1598810879&s=books&sr=1-1

[36] https://www.amazon.com/Emotional-Intelligence-2-0-Travis-Bradberry/dp/0974320625/ref=sr_1_3?dchild=1&keywords=emotional+intelligence+2.0&qid=1605559502&s=books&sr=1-3

confidential EQ assessment as well as direction to specific strategies to increase your EQ.

A Leader's Legacy[37] by James Kouzes and Barry Posner – Every leader wants to leave a legacy, but few take the time to reflect on how they'll be remembered. Legacy, as defined by Kouzes and Posner, is not only about making a difference but also focusing on what you leave behind. This book is a series of essays that offer guidance in choosing your own leadership legacy.

Leadership and Self-Deception (getting out of the box)[38] by The Arbinger Institute – Told through a fable, *Leadership and Self-Deception* demonstrates that the way we view others (as people or objects) influences our thinking and, more importantly, our behaviors at home, at work, and in the world. The frequency and speed at which our minds take us through this process is astounding. Getting out of our own boxes can change lives, improve relationships, and reshape organizations.

---

[37] https://www.amazon.com/Leaders-Legacy-James-M-Kouzes/dp/0787982962/ref=sr_1_1?dchild=1&keywords=a+leader%27s+legacy&qid=1605559682&s=books&sr=1-1

[38] https://www.amazon.com/Leadership-Self-Deception-Getting-Out-Box/dp/1523097809/ref=sr_1_2?crid=355RYV1SBU1CE&dchild=1&keywords=leadership+and+self+deception+by+the+arbinger+institute&qid=1605559727&s=books&sprefix=leadersihp%2Cstripbooks%2C206&sr=1-2

The 5 Second Rule[39] by Mel Robbins – Are you stuck or stalled in any part of your life? Learning how to use the simple 5 Second Rule method will get you up and going. Once you get started, nothing will stop you. Run, don't walk, if procrastination is where you live. Mel provides story after story of the life-changing moments the 5 Second Rule has inspired.

The Power of Moments[40] by Chip Heath & Dan Heath – What makes a moment truly memorable? Why do these moments stand out in our minds from others? How can we have more memorable moments? Defining moments have at least one of these elements: "elevation" (going beyond expectations), "insight" (learning something new about oneself), "pride" (feeling personal fulfilment), or "connection" (sharing the moment with another person).

The Power of TED (The Empowerment Dynamic)[41] by David Emerald – Emerald brings us a fable about self-leadership that focuses on taking ourselves out of the role of victim and into the role of creator. The Empowerment Dynamic is a formula for changing our focus from what we *don't want* to what we *do want* in our lives. Understanding how we

---

[39] https://www.amazon.com/Second-Rule-Transform-Confidence-Everyday/dp/1682612384/ref=sr_1_2?crid=16DOFVE9WS005&dchild=1&keywords=the+5+second+rule+by+mel+robbins&qid=1605559822&s=books&sprefix=the+5+second+rule%2Cstripbooks%2C237&sr=1-2

[40] https://www.amazon.com/Power-Moments-Certain-Experiences-Extraordinary/dp/1501147765/ref=sr_1_2?dchild=1&keywords=the+power+of+moments&qid=1605559879&s=books&sr=1-2

[41] https://www.amazon.com/POWER-TED-EMPOWERMENT-DYNAMIC-Anniversary/dp/0996871802/ref=sr_1_1?dchild=1&keywords=the+power+of+TED&qid=1605559963&s=books&sr=1-1

view ourselves in the world (as a victim or a creator) helps us to enable and embrace change, learning, and growth.

Search Inside Yourself[42] by Chade-Meng Tan – Tan calls himself the "jolly good fellow of Google." As an engineer and creator of the course, "Search Inside Yourself," he shares his wit and wisdom on how meditation/mindfulness practices can provide a platform for creativity, innovation, emotional intelligence, and, of course, world peace (Tan's ultimate goal). With a mix of humor, science, and easy-to-follow exercises, we can all become more self-aware and compassionate towards our co-workers, families, friends, and the planet.

The Silent Language of Leaders[43] by Carol Kinsey Goman – As much as our words, body language speaks volumes in the workplace. Personal space, gestures, posture, facial expressions, and even eye contact are strategic to managing, leading, motivating, and communicating clearly. Leaders need to be aware of how they present themselves every day and how their body language supports their message. Understanding the nuances of body language is critical to successfully navigating the thin line between success and failure as a leader.

---

[42] https://www.amazon.com/Search-Inside-Yourself-Unexpected-Achieving/dp/0062116932/ref=sr_1_1?crid=2DXNSYFPUFAKN&dchild=1&keywords=search+inside+yourself+chade+meng+tan&qid=1605560042&s=books&sprefix=search+inside+y%2Cstripbooks%2C219&sr=1-1

[43] https://www.amazon.com/Silent-Language-Leaders-Help-Hurt-How/dp/0470876360/ref=sr_1_3?dchild=1&keywords=silent+language+of+leaders&qid=1605560093&s=books&sr=1-3

StrengthsFinder 2.0[44] by Tom Rath – Validate your talents and strengths through an online assessment and learn how your strengths serve you. *StrenghthsFinder 2.0* will help you identify opportunities to do what you do best every day and increase your engagement, creativity, and pleasure in work and life!

Triggers[45] by Marshall Goldsmith and Mark Reiter – Goldsmith brings us a book that is devoted to helping us make behavioral changes that will get us to the next level. He provides us with six questions that can help to create focus as well as a specific structure and process to maintain accountability. An easy read with the promise of moving us from planning to doing.

Untamed[46] by Glennon Doyle – "The braver we are, the luckier we get." *Untamed* is the story, told through a memoir, of how we can begin to trust ourselves enough to set boundaries, make peace with our bodies, honor our anger and heartbreak, and unleash our deepest instincts to become who we are meant to be.

---

[44] https://www.amazon.com/StrengthsFinder-2-0-Tom-Rath/dp/159562015X/ref=sr_1_1?crid=2YY0H748HQFVB&dchild=1&keywords=strengthsfinder+2.0+with+access+code&qid=1598037071&sprefix=strengthsfinder%2Caps%2C1173&sr=8-1

[45] https://www.amazon.com/Triggers-audiobook/dp/B00UKE4ZZ2/ref=sr_1_1?crid=15UZEFTEJU50Q&dchild=1&keywords=triggers+marshall+goldsmith&qid=1605560199&s=books&sprefix=triggers+mar%2Cstripbooks%2C251&sr=1-1

[46] https://www.amazon.com/Untamed-Glennon-Doyle-Melton/dp/1984801252/ref=sr_1_1?dchild=1&keywords=untamed&qid=1598810207&sr=8-1

When[47] by Daniel Pink – Pink takes us through the science of timing to answer the question, "when?" When is the best time to work, nap, exercise, take a test, have surgery, and much more. He provides us with the research behind the answers as well as practical guidance to find our own best timing in life.

---

[47] https://www.amazon.com/When-Scientific-Secrets-Perfect-Timing/dp/0735210632/ref=tmm_pap_swatch_0?_encoding=UTF8&qid=1605560243&sr=1-1

APPENDIX B
5 TIPS TO COMBAT AGEISM

Mature job seekers often point to ageism (age discrimination) as the reason why they didn't get the screening call, get past the first interview or, in the end, get the job offer. While age discrimination in the job search process does exist, here are five factors that you, as a mature job seeker, can focus on to limit or eliminate the impact of ageism.

1. If you think ageism is the reason that you didn't get the job offer, think about culture and fit.

    A senior level job seeker, who was applying for a controller job at a non-profit, sat through a panel interview with a group of millennials. He came away from the interview knowing that if he were offered the job, he would turn it down. He knew that he wouldn't be comfortable in an organization where he was old enough to be everyone's father. What he took away from this experience was the importance of culture. He had the credentials and the qualifications to do the job, but the fit was wrong. (see "Exercise Your Core Values" – page 53).

2. If you think ageism is the reason you that didn't get the job offer, think about your appearance.

    With most interviews being conducted virtually, make the necessary adjustments to your camera to highlight your best side (consider lighting and background). Stand up when you are interviewing. Not only will you feel more energized, but your self-confidence will rise, and your voice will be stronger and your gestures more natural. Consider updating your appearance — makeup, hairstyle, glasses, and clothing, etc. Start a health regimen aimed at losing a few pounds and getting in a bit better shape. These simple changes will improve your outlook and give you a more youthful appearance.

3. If you think ageism is the reason you that did not get the job offer, think about value.

What value do you bring to potential employers? Your task is to sell your industry experience, your wisdom, and your adaptability as well as your ability to hit the ground running. Seasoned workers are excellent teachers and mentors who bring a worldview and best practices that can benefit a new employer. How are you showcasing your value?

4. If you think ageism is the reason you that did not get the job offer, think through the direction of your career.

Now is the time to gain clarity on your employment window and your career trajectory. Start by answering this list of questions:

- Will your next job continue to move you up the ladder of responsibility?
- Are you willing to take a lower-level position to spend more time with your family and work at a more relaxed pace?
- Are you willing to be a team member instead of a team leader?
- Does being the resident expert appeal to you?

- What are the income requirements for your next job?
- Are benefits more important than salary?

Answering these questions will guide your search and delineate your career goals.

5. If you think ageism is the reason that you did not get the job offer, think about filling in employment gaps.

   Is there a growing gap in your employment history? If so, consider looking for project, contract, or volunteer work. Project or contract work can give an employer a method to evaluate your skills and abilities while providing you with an income. In addition, project work can help you keep your skills fresh and could ultimately lead to a job offer. Similarly, volunteer work can provide networking opportunities while closing the hole in your resume.

By implementing these 5 tips, your age will be an advantage rather than a roadblock on your career journey.

Resources for job seekers over 50

Nfifty50s.com: Nifty50s offer news and advice for older workers and job seekers over 50.

www.retirementjobs.com: The goal of Retirement Jobs is to identify companies who welcome older workers and match them with active, productive, conscientious, mature adults seeking a job or project that matches their lifestyle.

www.retiredbrains.com: Retired Brains is a comprehensive and independent resource that specializes in helping baby boomers, those planning their retirements, and active retirees. be happy, healthy and prosperous. Information covers quality of life, financial stability, and opportunities for continued growth.

AARP Job Search[48] - The AARP Job Board was designed to help you match your years of valuable experience with employers who are committed to an age-diverse workforce.

www.seniorjobbank.org: Senior Job Bank brings together employers with qualified older job seekers.

www.seniors4hire.org: Senior 4 Hire advocates for seniors seeking jobs or other ways to earn a living. This resource works to persuade businesses to overcome any vestiges of age discrimination, while providing content that prepares job seekers to compete with confidence in the recruitment marketplace.

---

[48] http://jobs.aarp.org/

Appendix C
JOB SEARCH GROUPS ACROSS THE US

In a job search group, you will surround yourself with the support, encouragement, and inspiration of other job seekers. Sharing time with other job seekers can help you get your own job search started, maintain your momentum, and accelerate the success. You will feel more productive and ramp up your skills throughout the search process.

NATIONWIDE DIRECTORY

https://www.briefcasecoach.com/jobsearchgroups/ – Sarah Johnston, the Briefcase Coach, created a nationwide directory of Job Search Groups. The groups listed below are additions to her directory.

California

https://workforce.org/jobseekers/ *(San Diego, California)*

San Diego Workforce Partnerships – *We have tools and information to help you:*

- Identify career opportunities that align with your strengths and interests

- Find training programs and live job postings
- Use labor market information to make informed training and career decisions

https://thejobforum.org/ *(San Francisco, California)*
Free Job Search Advice from Local Business Managers – *Coaching job hunters and providing job search advice in virtual sessions every Wednesday and Thursday evenings for free*

Colorado

http://www.collectivenet.org/ *(Colorado)*

CollectiveNet is a non-profit umbrella organization of career networking groups designed to maximize job seeking and employee search efforts by providing a central location of candidates, contacts, leads and information with no fees associated and volunteer operated.

CollectiveNet targets jobseekers and employers in an effective, efficient, and productive method that is results-driven and based on honesty, integrity, and cooperation.

Florida

https://tbjl.org/ *(Tampa, Florida)*

Tampa Bay Job Links (TBJL) is a non-profit organization that provides individuals with career and job-search coaching, and local employers with qualified candidates.

Illinois

https://careervision.org/chicago-area-job-search-groups/ *(Chicago, Illinois)*

Career Vision is an excellent starting point for locating job search support groups in the greater Chicago area.

https://thebarringtoncareercenter.org/ *(Chicago, Illinois)*

The Barrington Career Center is a volunteer driven, non-profit agency dedicated to helping clients develop search strategies, skills, and conduct an effective job search. Unemployment, underemployment, career transition, re-entry to the workforce, or first-time employment are all areas where we can help.

Indiana

https://www.golove.org/passport *(Indianapolis, Indiana)*

Passport to Employment is a thriving employment ministry program designed to support, encourage, and equip those who are on a journey to new or better employment.

http://www.indyatwork.com/jobseeker-central/job-clubs/ *(Indianapolis, Indiana)*

Like networking groups, "job clubs" are organizations solely devoted to people in career transition.

http://www.b-p-e.org/ *(Indiana - 7 chapters throughout state)*

Business & Professional Exchange empowers you take control of your job search by connecting you with people who can help by offering a variety of services and opportunities for career professionals seeking re-employment.

Kentucky

https://www.ukalumni.net/jobclub *(Lexington, Kentucky)*

Looking to make a career transition? Are you underemployed or out of work? Central Kentucky Job Club is a free workshop open to the public and brought to you by The University of Kentucky Alumni Association, Fayette County Cooperative Extension Service, and the UK Human Resources STEPS Temporary Employment. Job Club meets the 2nd and 4th Tuesday of each month.

Missouri

http://bbj.org/ *(St Louis, Missouri)*

Businesspersons Between Jobs, known as BBJ, is a non-denominational job search support group assisting unemployed and underemployed people at different stages of their careers. We have been proudly serving the St. Louis community for over 40 years.

What makes us unique? Members of the BBJ community, including our staff, have experienced unemployment and the challenge of job loss. As a result, we have developed a dedicated community focused on getting you back to work quickly.

North Carolina

https://www.meetup.com/Triangle-Executive-Careers-Group/ - *(Raleigh, North Carolina)*

The Triangle Executive Careers Group, provides members with the information, support, and tools they need to take charge of their careers, find jobs they love, earn what they deserve and reach their work life mission.

https://jobsearching.org/meetings/ *(Winston Salem, North Carolina)*

The Winston Salem Chapter of Professionals in Transition® meets weekly to serve North Carolina's Triad Region! It is affectionately referred to as The Roger Pike Memorial Chapter. Charter member Roger Pike served PIT® with distinction for 18 years until his passing in 2010.

Ohio

https://jsfg.com/ *(Cincinnati, Ohio)*

Job Search Focus Group Cincinnati (Hyde Park) is an all-volunteer, non-denominational outreach for professionals in career transition. JSFG members successfully navigate their career transition or job search through purposeful networking — connecting and building business relationships in an encouraging and supportive environment.

Oregon & Washington

https://www.macslist.org/ *(Pacific North West — Portland & Seattle)*

Mac's List connects job seekers and employers, so together they can make better employment decisions, grow successful organizations, and build meaningful careers. We do this with educational resources, local professional-level job listings, and community-building activities.

Pennsylvania

https://www.wcjp.org/ *(West Central, Pennsylvania)*

West Central Job Partnership - We understand that finding a first job, changing careers, or starting over in the workforce is not easy. Individualized services allow the PA CareerLink® staff to meet the needs of each person that comes through our doors. We can help you regardless of your educational background, work history, prior training, or current employment.

Tennessee

https://knoxworx.klf.org/job-clubs/ *(Knoxville, Tennessee)*

Not everyone enters the employment process at the same level. Maybe you have a degree and/or skills but are having a hard time navigating the job market and getting connected with the right people.

KnoxWorx Job Clubs meet regularly around Knoxville to encourage and inform job seekers by sharing job search ideas, offering networking opportunities, and providing constructive discussion with people who understand what is involved in a career transition.

https://bumc.net/care/careertransitions/ *(Nashville, Tennessee)*

Career Transitions helps people who are in-between jobs or looking for a career change by offering weekly presentations focused on the latest job search techniques.

Our presenters are highly experienced human resources professionals and recruiters, with many nationally known experts in the area of job seeking. Topics include resume writing, interviewing skills, networking, setting goals, creating a target list of potential employers, negotiation, and much more.

Virginia

https://saint-mikes.org/jobs-assistance-ministry (Richmond, Virginia)

JAM is open to all who seek help finding a job. The ministry offers an immense amount of resources and is free to anyone who may have been out of a job for some time, is seeking to make a career transition, or has just lost a job. Through resume reviews, mock interviews, networking, coaching, and workshops, so many have found employment through this wonderful ministry.

ACKNOWLEDGMENTS

I would like to acknowledge the help and backing of friends, colleagues, and family who cheered on my efforts in writing, editing, and publishing this book. Special thanks go out to:

- Robert Lazarow, my husband, for being a passionate supporter and a loving partner.
- Katherine Burik, The Interview Doctor, for sharing her publishing expertise.
- Mike Segal and Steve Tomasko, and the members of the Summit Networking Group for enabling me to share their job search obstacles, their questions, and their stories.
- Nick Bavaro, James T. Boggs, Paul DiPronio, and JB Bryant who gave of their time to review my first draft and offer their edits, corrections, and comments.
- Richard Fox, David Skoglund, and Lamar Ratcliff for sharing their insights, their feedback, and their wisdom.
- Those who generously (and anonymously) shared their job search stories.

REFERENCES

Achor, S. (2013). *Before Happiness.* New York, NY: Crown Business.

Adams, M. P. (2015). *Change your Questions, Change your Life: 12 powerful tools for leadership, coaching, and life.* Oakland, CA: Berrett-Koehler Publishers, Inc.

Baker, W. (2020). *All You Have to Do Is Ask: How to master the most important skill for success.* New York: Currency Books.

Brown, B. (2015). *Rising Strong: The reckoning. The rumble. The revolution.* New York: Random House.

Burfoot, A. (2019, June 30). *There's Now Research to Back the Trend Toward Scorn of Processed Foods.* Washington, DC, US. Retrieved from https://www.sciencealert.com/there-s-now-research-to-back-the-trend-of-scorn-towards-processed-food

Clear, J. (2019). *Atomic Habits: An easy & proven way to build good habits & break bad ones.* New York: Penguin Random House.

Doyle, G. (2013, May 31). *Lessons from the Mental Hospital.* Retrieved from TedX.

Kessler, D. A. (2010). *The End of Overeating: Taking control of the insatiable American Appetite.* New York: Rodale Books.

Kubler-Ross, E. (1969). *On Death and Dying: what the dying have to teach doctors, nurses, clergy & their own families.* New York, NY: Scribner.

Maxwell, J. (2014). *Good Leaders Ask Great Questions.* Center Street.

Mrosko, T. (2014, December 31). Nine Elements of Resiliency. *Cleveland Plain Dealer.*

Nelson, P. (1993). *There's a Hole in my Sidewalk: The romance of self-discovery.* Hillsboro, OR: Beyond Words Publishing, Inc.

Sandberg, S., & Grant, A. (2017). *Option B: Facing adversity, building resilience, and finding joy.* New York, New York: Alfred A Knopf.

Seery, M. D. (2011). Resilience: A silver lining to experiencing adverse life events? *Current Directions in Psychological Science, 20*(6), 390-394.

TapRoot Root Cause Analysis. (2013, April 11). Retrieved from www.taproot.com: https://www.taproot.com/live-your-core-values-exercise-to-increase-your-success/

ABOUT THE AUTHOR

Marsha Friedman, MLS, RCC[TM], DTM, is the principal and founder of *MEF Consulting Group*.[49] As a leadership and personal development coach, Marsha works with mid-level managers and small business owners to improve leadership effectiveness, reduce workplace drama, and drive retention and engagement.

Prior to founding MEF Consulting Group, Marsha was the head of learning and organization development for Diebold Global Service Logistics. Her 30+-year career at Diebold spanned across the organization from finance to customer service, and from operations to organizational development.

Marsha co-facilitates Summit Networking Group for executive-level job seekers. She is the author of Surviving and Thriving Despite the Drama: 7 Remarkable Strategies to Regain Control, Develop Resilience, and Rewrite Your Own Happily Ever After Ending.[50]

In her free time, Marsha enjoys cooking and sharing meals with family

---

[49] http://www.consultmef.com/

[50] https://www.amazon.com/Surviving-Thriving-Despite-Drama-Happily-Ever-After-ebook/dp/B07R2C4YNC/ref=sr_1_1?crid=K87DJITPB25V&dchild=1&keywords=surviving+and+thriving+despite+the+drama&qid=1597859421&sprefix=surviving+and+thriving+despite%2Caps%2C253&sr=8-1

and friends, and working out. She is passionate about live theater and films, dark chocolate, and good wine! Marsha and her husband, Bob, have 4 children, 10 grandchildren, and a tabby cat named Mingo.

Speaker Information

Looking for a speaker or trainer who can connect with everyone in your audience?

Then look no further! Marsha engages her audiences with her natural humor and charm and "is a clear and articulate speaker who is able to connect with a wide variety of audiences."

Marsha's most popular topics include:

- **Benefits of Failure:** Turn Your Greatest Failures into Your Greatest Successes
- **Your Full Potential:** The 6 Practices You Need to Stop and the 6 Practices You Need to Start to Reach Your Full Potential.
- **Resilience – The Magic Ingredient:** How to Overcome the Roadblocks That Life Throws Your Way.
- **Connecting the Dots:** Personal Value Propositions: The Key to Increasing Engagement and Productivity

Marsha is available for both live and online events. Your audience members will gain valuable insights and actionable takeaways that they can use immediately.

Book Marsha Friedman today by contacting her at: 330-603-1890 or marsha@consultmef.com or visit consultmef.com.

What Other Event Planners Say

About Working with Marsha…

"Marsha's ability to deliver training in an effective and engaging way was remarkable. Her unique gift of relating to a diverse group of people helped us deliver our program to hundreds of employees. Marsha is an invaluable resource whom we hope to partner with again the future!" **Manager of Talent Management, US Acute Care Solutions**

"Marsha's personalization of our education has been astronomical to our success. She is creative in her thinking, reliable, and consistently exceeded our expectations!" **Director of Quality and Risk Management, Summa Rehab Hospital**

"Marsha projects un-paralleled energy and confidence, making her messages distinct and relatable." **Director of Training, DRB Systems**

Book Marsha Friedman today by contacting her at: 330-603-1890 or marsha@consultmef.com.

To learn more about Marsha and MEF Consulting Group, LLC., visit www.linkedin.com/in/marshafriedman1 or www.consultmef.com.

www.ingramcontent.com/pod-product-compliance
Lightning Source LLC
Chambersburg PA
CBHW070658220526
45466CB00001B/487